DATE DUE

MAY 3 0 1994		
JUN 5 '95		
JUN 28 '95		
NOV 21 95		
NOV 18 '96		
DE 1 '97		
JV 15 '99		
MY 12 00		

```
976.4
St      Stewart, Gail
           Texans. By Gail Stewart.  Vero Beach,
        FL, Rourke Publications, Inc., c.1990.
           [32]p.  illus.  (The Wild West in
        American History)

             ISBN:0-86625-408-0


           1.Texas--History--To 1846.  I.Title.
        II.Series.
```

COLOMA PUBLIC LIBRARY

The Wild West in American History

Written by Gail Stewart
Illustrated by Joe Nordstrom
Edited by Mark E. Ahlstrom

© 1990 Rourke Publications, Inc.

All rights reserved. No part of this book may be reproduced or
utilized in any form or by any means, electronic or mechanical,
including photocopying, recording or by any information
storage and retrieval system without permission in writing
from the publisher.

LIBRARY OF CONGRESS
Library of Congress Cataloging-in-Publication Data

Stewart, Gail, 1949-
   Texans / by Gail B. Stewart.
     p. cm. -- (The Wild West in American history)
   Summary: Traces the turbulent history of the Lone Star State, recounting
the struggles of early Texas settlers and their battle for independence.
   ISBN 0-86625-408-0
   1. Texas--History--To 1846--Juvenile literature. [1. Texas--History--To 1846.]
I. Title. II. Series.
F389.S95 1990
976.4--dc20   89-37766
                                                                                 CIP
                                                                                   AC

Rourke Publications, Inc.
Vero Beach, Florida, 32964

TEXANS

TEXANS

If you had been alive in the 1820's and had been traveling with your family through the frontier of Kentucky or Tennessee, you might have come upon a puzzling thing. As you approached a tiny backwoods settlement, you would have been looking forward to meeting the settlers and talking to them. Many of these little frontier settlements, however, would have been empty—like ghost towns.

Curious, you might have gone up to one of the log cabins and looked around. In thick, black letters painted across the door you'd have seen the letters "GTT." You might have seen that same mysterious message on hundreds of cabins across the frontier. What did it mean? What had happened to the people? Had there been a violent Indian raid? Had the settlers scrawled some message, trying to warn those who came looking for them?

The answer was nothing so disastrous. The occupants of the cabins had left peacefully, of their own will. They had taken their few possessions and had left the frontier for a new place. The new place, said to be "more heavenly than even Kentucky," was supposed to be unbelievably huge. There was so much room, it was said, that millions of families could live there, yet never crowd one another.

As the families prepared to leave, they jubilantly painted a message on their doors. They wanted everyone to know that they had gone to a place where there were horses running wild, where there were fat cattle, and rich black soil for planting. "GTT," their message said—Gone to Texas!

A BLOODY AND VIOLENT PAST

More than any of the other states, Texas has had a painful history. Those who came from the American frontier to settle in Texas back in the early 1800's were intruding on another nation's territory. Over the centuries, the land that is now Texas has been fought over—pushed and pulled apart—by the United States, by Spain, and by Mexico. At the time the first American settlers arrived, Texas was owned by Spain.

In many ways, Texas' history is unique. For example, it is the only one of the 50 states that was an independent country, with its own president, before it became a state. The Texans were the first Americans to establish a settlement west of the Mississippi and Missouri rivers. These settlers didn't think of themselves as Americans, however. In fact, they insisted that they were first and foremost Texans. These Texans fought hard to be independent and free.

Today, when many people think of the Old West, they often think of Texas. They think of the cowboys, the rodeos, and the long, dusty cattle drives. They think, too, of the murdering outlaws and bandits who roamed the Texas plains.

What caused Texas to be a unique area in the Old West? Why was its history so violent? Who were these fiercely independent, proud people called Texans?

The history of Texas has been filled with violence. This painting shows fighting at the battle for the Alamo. (Art: University of Oklahoma.)

"THE FRIENDS" WERE FIRST

The first people who lived in what is now Texas were tribes of Indian people. Many centuries ago, there were about 30,000 Indians living in Texas, mainly in the eastern part. Most of these Indians belonged to the Caddo tribe. The Caddo Indians were peaceful, getting along with other Indian tribes in the area. The Caddos called themselves "Tejas," which means "the friends." It is from this ancient Indian word that the name "Texas" comes.

The first non-Indians to visit northern Mexico and Texas were Spanish explorers. The Spanish had sailed across the Atlantic in the early 16th century, searching for new lands. They were the first to map out the coastline of Texas and Mexico.

These Spanish explorers brought something with them that the Indians had never seen— horses. At that time, there were no horses at all in North America. Largely because of their

horses, the Spanish found it easy to control and dominate the Indians of the new territory. A man on horseback was far more powerful than a man on foot. By 1542, Mexico (including 268,000 square miles of Texas) was claimed by these Spanish invaders.

More and more Spaniards arrived in Mexico, and many of them settled in the northernmost part of Mexico—in an area already known as Texas. Many of these Spanish people were explorers searching for gold. There were legends, in those days, of seven beautiful cities made of gold. Anyone who was lucky enough to find these cities would be the richest person in the world. Not surprisingly, the lure of gold was so powerful that it made men leave their families and homes in Spain and make a dangerous journey across the sea.

Many of the Spaniards were religious missionaries. They felt it was important for them to spread their Catholic religion to the Indians of Mexico and Texas. For almost 300 years, Spanish priests and their helpers built missions, or large churches, throughout the country.

On their way to Texas, the Spanish explorers discovered—among other things—the Grand Canyon, in what is now the state of Arizona.

MOSES AUSTIN'S PLAN

On a sunny June morning in 1820, an American named Moses Austin was riding through east Texas. Austin was a businessman—had been, that is, until his Missouri business went bankrupt. Austin was not a lazy man, however, and he was eagerly searching for some new way to make money.

The Texas countryside seemed to him to have all sorts of possibilities. It was hard for Austin to imagine anyone who would not be excited by the Texas countryside! There was rich black soil, just right for farming. The forests and plains were alive with all sorts of game. There were crystal-clear rivers brimming with fish. Best of all, this was a land that was so big it seemed limitless. If he could somehow acquire some of this rich Texas land, Moses Austin thought to himself, he could surely sell it at a handsome profit.

Austin knew, however, that getting permission for Americans to settle in Texas would be difficult. The Spanish government in Mexico didn't trust Americans. The Spaniards thought of Americans as greedy for land, always wanting to push their boundaries farther and farther west. Already, more than one million settlers from the United States had pushed the frontier back over the Appalachian Mountains into Kentucky and Tennessee. It was just a matter of time, thought the Spanish, until the Americans cast their eyes on Texas. Any plan that Moses Austin presented to Spanish authorities in Mexico had to persuade the Spanish that they had nothing to fear from American settlers.

Just as Austin had predicted, the Spanish governor in San Antonio was suspicious of the idea. But Moses Austin had brought several good arguments with him. First of all, he assured the governor that the settlers would be people hand-selected by Austin himself. They would be law-abiding people. There would be no drunkards or lazy men. These settlers would be interested in making a good, decent living for themselves and their families.

Even more to the governor's liking, Austin promised that these settlers would give up their American citizenship. They would swear their loyalty to Mexico and the King of Spain. The Spanish government wouldn't have to worry that the Americans were eyeing Texas as a new possession to be added to the United States. Along with their allegiance to Spain, the new settlers would also adopt the Roman Catholic religion. Ever since the Spanish invaded Mexico in the 1500's, the national religion had been Catholicism. The new Americans wouldn't be any different from Spanish settlers, Austin assured the governor.

The governor thought the proposal over. A smart man, he knew that the Texas countryside was in need of settlers. Even though the Spanish owned Texas, fewer than 3,000 Spaniards had settled there. By having more permanent residents, Texas would be safer from Indian raids, as well as from intrusion from less law-abiding Americans. These American-turned-Spanish settlers of Austin's could help defend the land against unfriendly intruders. If Austin kept his word, what was the harm? The governor finally agreed, and Austin was told to begin choosing his settlers.

Before the Spanish came, there were no horses in North America! *(Art: Denver Public Library. Western History Dept.)*

A SON'S LOYALTY

Many historians say that if it weren't for the loyalty of Moses Austin's son, the story of Texas would have been far different. Moses died before any of the settling could take place. His deathbed wish was that his son Stephen would take over for him.

Stephen was not the robust, adventurous man his father was. He preferred reading and playing his flute to organizing large groups of people. He was, however, willing to continue with his father's plans, so he set to work right away. He sent announcements throughout the settlements of the American frontier that land was available to certain people to be chosen by him.

The response was, as Moses Austin had imagined, overwhelming. Everyone who had heard about the vast land of Texas wanted to be a part of it. Austin spent a lot of time answering hundreds of letters from eager settlers. In the end, he chose 300 families. These have been called by historians "The Old Three Hundred." Each family received its choice of land—either 177 acres of farmland, or 4,428 acres of good grazing land for cattle. The settlement was started on the banks of the Brazos River, around a town they called San Felipe de Austin.

Very soon after the settlers arrived, they received word from far-away Mexico City that there had been a revolution. The Mexican people, long resentful of their Spanish overlords, had overthrown the government. Mexico, which had been a possession of Spain for the last 300 years, was now independent.

This was to change things for the transplanted Americans at San Felipe de Austin, but not right away. For the time being, the new government of Mexico was pleased to allow settlers from America to move into Texas. They wouldn't be Spanish citizens, however—they were pledged to Mexico.

Stephen Austin spent many hours patiently writing letters to eager settlers.

A GROWING SETTLEMENT

With Mexico's encouragement, therefore, more and more American settlers poured into the Texas territory. Their numbers grew quickly—to more than 10,000 by 1827. In the next three years, that number would double—to 20,000 settlers!

The settlers came from many places in America. Some came from the original 13 states. Others came from the frontiers of Kentucky, Ohio, Tennessee, and Illinois. A large number of the new Texans were Southerners. They came to plant cotton in the rich Texas soil. Since this was a time before slavery was abolished, many of the Southern farmers had slaves, and they brought these slaves with them to Texas.

Cotton was not the only crop that grew well in Texas. Farmers also planted corn and sugarcane. They raised cattle, too. The work was backbreaking, and the days seemed endless. Yet the settlement continued to prosper and grow.

Most of the settlers lived in log cabins, very much like the ones frontiersmen built in Kentucky. As their crops grew and money became more plentiful, however, they built finer homes. Historians tell us that many of the settlers built houses like the ones they had had before moving to Texas. These homes reflected their ethnic heritage. For instance, there were some strong, sturdy German homes. There were homes that looked very much like miniature plantation homes of the South. There were homes that looked like they belonged in Boston or New York. Texas was like a patchwork quilt of many different neighborhoods!

GROWING RESENTMENT

As the years went on, however, the Mexican government began to have uncomfortable feelings toward the Texans. They saw that the Americans were becoming a large majority in the Texas territory. If the Americans mounted an attack against the Mexicans in Texas, the Mexican government thought they would probably succeed. This made the Mexican government nervous, even though there hadn't been any reason to suspect the Texans would fight against the government.

On the contrary, the settlers had been of real service to the Mexicans. They had fought off Indians and American outlaws and criminals, just as Moses Austin had promised. Stephen Austin had worked very hard, keeping small problems from becoming big ones. He had acted as a go-between in many instances, to keep relations between Mexico and the Texans peaceful.

Yet the Mexican government found fault with some things the settlers had done. For one thing, Mexicans believed that slavery was wrong. They had forbidden all citizens to hold slaves, yet some of the Texans continued to keep them. Many of the Americans also agreed that slavery was wrong. However, they felt that the Mexican government had no right to interfere with a person's right to own slaves. What seems to us now to be a clear-cut case of wrongdoing was not so easy to see in those days. For the Texans, slavery wasn't the issue—it was a question of who had the right to tell them what to do.

Part of Mexico's nervousness about Texas was due to its own shaky situation. Since declaring its independence from Spain in 1821, Mexico had had its government change hands several times. When a nation declares its independence after many years of outside rule, it is often weak and easily upset. This was the case with Mexico. There were simply too many people who wanted power. These people saw the weak condition of the Mexican government as an invitation to seize that power for themselves.

Because Mexico was quite busy with its own problems, the government had little time to keep an eye on the Texans. That was fine with most of the Texans. They loved their independence. However, there were changes that occurred because of the lack of supervision.

One of these was the large numbers of "illegal" American settlers. These people had not been selected by Austin—they came simply because they wanted to claim some of what Texas had to offer. While many of these settlers were fine people, many others were troublemakers. They urged other settlers to fight the Mexicans, and grab Texas for themselves. This kind of thinking caused more problems with the worried Mexican government. In 1830, the Mexican government decided to cancel the deal that had been made with Austin. No more settlers from the United States would be allowed to move into Texas.

The Mexican government didn't like the fact that some Texans used slaves to work on their farms.

Despite problems, settlers and Indians often got along well. *(Photo: University of Oklahoma.)*

"THE NAPOLEON OF THE WEST"

In the early 1830's, the relationship between Texans and the Mexican government turned even more sour. The reason for this was the new Mexican ruler, Antonio Lopez de Santa Anna. Santa Anna had been the general of Mexico's army for a long time. In 1833, however, he decided that the time had come to seize control of the entire government. He led a revolt which resulted in all power resting solely with him. Santa Anna was now the military dictator of Mexico.

Santa Anna was a handsome, striking man. He had had great success as a general in rousing his men to victory in the most difficult situations. Santa Anna enjoyed parading around in the most lavish, colorful uniforms he could find. Each of his many uniforms was covered with gold and silver medals.

Santa Anna thought of himself as more than the leader of a nation. He was fond of saying, "Men are nothing; power is everything." He was so hungry for power, in fact, that he was known as the "Napoleon of the West," after the famous French general. Santa Anna had no patience at all for anyone who tried to limit his power.

That was, however, what the Texans were trying to do, although they never said that in so many words. The Texans were angry that the government had closed the door on American immigration. They urged Santa Anna to reconsider that decision.

The Texans had other demands, too. They wanted to be allowed some "home rule"—the right to establish their own laws and court system. Mexico City, the capital of Mexico, was terribly far away from Texas. Communication between the two places was cumbersome and slow. The Texans wanted to know why they couldn't handle their own problems. Stephen Austin traveled to Mexico City with a list of the Texans' ideas. Would Santa Anna and his government respect the Texans enough to listen?

Santa Anna was fond of fancy uniforms.

THE LAST STRAW

Not only did Austin fail to persuade Santa Anna to give Texans more freedoms—Austin lost his own! Mexican soldiers seized Austin on his journey back to Texas and threw him into jail. Without a trial or any way to defend himself, Austin was accused of plotting against the Mexican government. He would sit in that same jail for the next one-and-a-half years.

The settlers back in Texas had had enough. They were outraged, and began talking of war against the Mexicans. Many of the settlers wanted to grab their rifles and set out the very day they heard about Austin's capture, but others protested. Surely, they thought, Santa Anna could be reasoned with. Perhaps it would still be possible to keep peace between Texans and the Mexican government.

The settlers hoping for peace, however, soon

realized that war could not be avoided. They received word that Santa Anna was soon going to march north from Mexico City with tens of thousands of soldiers. He was planning on teaching the Texans a lesson.

In the meantime, though, Santa Anna sent another general, his brother-in-law Martin Perfecto de Cos. Cos lead a small army to the Texas town of Gonzales. His job was to seize a small brass cannon that the settlers had been given years before. The cannon was used by the settlers of that little town to fight off Indians.

It wasn't so much that the cannon was important, historians tell us. It was just Santa Anna's way of telling the Texans they were no longer to be trusted with weapons. Cos and his men were to take the cannon, thereby showing "a little muscle" to the Texans. Such a show of force, thought Santa Anna, might make the Texans rethink their talk about independence.

While on his way back to Texas, Austin was captured and thrown into jail by the Mexicans.

"COME AND TAKE IT!"

The hundred or so cavalry soldiers with Cos weren't expecting much of a problem with the job at hand. In fact, they weren't really all that interested. Many of the soldiers were criminals, released from jail only to help in military service. They weren't trained fighters, nor particularly good shots with their rifles. They were poorly fed and poorly clothed men who didn't have much at stake.

On the other hand, the Texans at Gonzales were ready for battle. They had hung a big sign on the cannon which said: "Come and Get It!" The eager settlers waited, fingers on triggers, for the Mexican troops to storm into town.

The "battle" was over almost instantly. All it took, in fact, was one loud blast from the cannon, and the Mexican troops fled in panic. The Texans were torn between disappointment and excitement. The disappointment was because the fight had been so boring—it was over almost before it began. The excitement was because a revolution had truly begun. There was no turning back now. Texas had, in no uncertain terms, declared its independence from Mexico.

SAM HOUSTON, A LEADER

The Texans were going to fight, and they needed a commander. The overwhelming choice was a former governor of Tennessee, Sam Houston.

Houston had come to Texas a few years before, as a favor to President Andrew Jackson. Jackson had wanted a reliable pair of eyes and ears on the Texas frontier, to keep track of the situation there. Houston had arrived in Texas just in time to see the crumbling relations with Santa Anna. He, too, agreed that war was inevitable.

The first thing Houston did was to seek out more troops for his army. He wrote letters to people back East, and put announcements in the newspapers. "Come to Texas," he urged. "Bring a good rifle and help us!" He promised that after Santa Anna was driven back to Mexico, all the volunteers who helped the Texans would be rewarded with land.

The volunteers poured in. The army's numbers were growing larger by the week. Some of the volunteers had fought before, but many were new at the whole thing. What they lacked in polish and experience, however, they more than made up for in enthusiasm. To almost all of these men, the fighting was a matter of pride and honor. They were protecting their way of life and their future.

With one blast of the Gonzales cannon, the battle was over!

**General Sam Houston
(Photo: University of Oklahoma.)**

NO WAITING FOR ORDERS

Unfortunately, the Texans' zeal and enthusiasm would get them into quite a bit of trouble. Instead of waiting for their commander to give them orders, this Texas army gave themselves an order. They simply set out from Gonzales and headed west, to San Antonio.

Houston was elsewhere when his army decided to attack Cos' army, which was now in San Antonio. He thought it was a foolish idea, but he knew very well that he couldn't stop the troops. They were simply too riled up and spoiling for a fight.

Once again, the Texans won. After five days of fighting, Cos waved the white flag signaling surrender. The Texans made Cos promise never to show his face in Texas again, and let him go.

By this time, the army was even wilder. They felt that they had virtually won the war. "Santa Anna wouldn't dare show his face in Texas now!" crowed the jubilant men. Houston tried to reason with them. He cautioned them that Santa Anna was bound to lead his massive army north to Texas. The war was not over, not by a long shot.

The ragtag Texas army didn't listen. They told Houston that even if Santa Anna came to Texas, he'd get the fight of his life. They could beat any army, no matter how large, they said. They were Texans, they reminded Houston and other worried leaders. After all, Texans could always win, no matter what the odds.

After five days of fighting, the Mexicans surrendered.

The main plaza of San Antonio as it appeared in 1850, a few years after the fighting.
(Photo: University of Oklahoma.)

READY FOR A FIGHT?

The Texans left a small "skeleton" army in San Antonio. The rest of the men went on, looking for more Mexican troops to fight. Houston felt it was foolish to remain in San Antonio, so he ordered his men to leave. He was sure that Santa Anna's army would be coming any day, and that the little Texas army left in San Antonio would be in danger. The other Texans ignored Houston's advice. Nothing would please them more than to take on Santa Anna himself. They would stay right where they were.

The small army of Texas settlers left in San Antonio camped in an old Spanish mission called the Alamo. It was built like a fort, with walls surrounding a courtyard. As word spread about the revolution, more and more men came to help out at the Alamo. They believed in the Texans' cause, and wanted to be in on the fight with the dictator Santa Anna.

Davy Crockett, about whom legends were already being told, brought some fighting men from Tennessee. Crockett had grown tired of his frontier of Tennessee—it was becoming more and more crowded. He had heard wonderful things about Texas, and moved west quickly. He wanted to be there, he said, to get in on the fun with Santa Anna.

Jim Bowie was another well-known hero at the Alamo. A native of Louisiana, Bowie had become legendary by riding on the backs of alligators in the Louisiana swamps. He was known as a brave, intelligent man. Although Bowie was deathly ill from pneumonia at the time, he tried hard to keep his men's spirits up.

Bowie was the inventor of the famous Bowie knife—called by some "the best knife in the world." It was curved, and the razor-sharp blade went the whole length of the knife—quite a change from the knives of the day that were sharp only on the end. The Bowie knife was used for skinning deer and bears, and fighting. There were more than a few Bowie knives present at the Alamo!

The oldest part of the Alamo—the church—was built in 1718.

Davy Crockett *(Art: University of Oklahoma.)*

Jim Bowie *(Photo: University of Oklahoma.)*

"REMEMBER THE ALAMO!"

Santa Anna arrived in San Antonio on February 23, 1836. As Sam Houston had predicted, Santa Anna was furious. He was determined to defeat the Texans who had defeated General Cos and his army. The first thing Santa Anna did was to hoist a red flag from the tower of a nearby church. That was a signal to the Texans to surrender or be killed. There would be no prisoners.

The small army of 163 Texans looked at the Mexican army of 5,000. They knew their chances were slim, but they felt that justice was on their side. They fired the first shot at Santa Anna's forces, and the battle began.

It was a one-way fight almost from the beginning. Santa Anna and his men were in no hurry—they had the advantage of more than enough ammunition. All the while, the Mexican army band played a death march called

Although it is not known exactly how Jim Bowie died, legend has it that he fought to the finish—as he lay sick in bed!

"Deguello" outside the walls of the Alamo. The Texans fought off several assaults. By March 6, however, they had run out of ammunition.

As Santa Anna and his men stormed the Alamo for the last time, the Texans tried to fight as best they could. They fought with the butts of their rifles and with knives, but there was no hope. The battle lasted only 90 minutes; all of the Texans were killed. Some historians say that an officer's wife and her small child were spared. Others note that a young black boy survived. The blood and death were everywhere, however. Davy Crockett lay slumped over his rifle. Jim Bowie was killed as he lay sick in his bed.

While the fighting at the Alamo was going on, Sam Houston and other leaders were writing a declaration of Texas' independence. The words were stirring and beautiful. When the leaders heard about the deaths of all those Texas fighters, it didn't seem to matter much, though.

WITH TEARS IN THEIR EYES

Santa Anna's troops were triumphant. They had proven they were the stronger army. The large force left San Antonio and went on to defeat another group of Texans at the town of Goliad. In Goliad, Santa Anna lived up to his reputation as a cruel general by slaughtering 393 Texans who had surrendered.

When word of the atrocity got out, settlers all over Texas were furious. It seemed as if Santa Anna had been given free rein to roam through Texas with his huge army. Everywhere he went, he slaughtered more and more people. The Texans wanted a fight. They wanted revenge for the killing of the men at the Alamo and at Goliad.

Sam Houston was ready to take control. He knew his army of ragtag frontiersmen didn't stand a chance quite yet. His idea was to buy some time for his army, waiting until just the right moment to make his move.

For one thing, extra time would give more volunteers a chance to join the army. The newspapers in the United States had been full of stories of the heroes at the Alamo. More and more men were coming to help—they knew the fighting wasn't over yet. For another thing, Houston was experienced enough to know that Santa Anna would eventually make a mistake—all generals do. If he could avoid fighting until the Mexicans had their guard down, he and his army might have a chance.

This strategy angered and confused his men. They thought he was being a coward. Many of them wept openly; one man later said the army was marching with tears in their eyes. They had come to fight. What was wrong with Sam Houston?

Some speculated that he had lost his nerve. Many felt he was drinking whiskey on the sly, and that it was making his judgment poor. But Houston stuck with his plan to avoid a fight until his army was ready.

At least part of his strategy was working. With each passing day his ragtag army was slowly getting bigger. Finally Houston felt that his army was ready to take on Santa Anna. He knew he couldn't win a full-scale battle, but he thought that a surprise attack would be successful. Houston would have to be careful to wait for the right moment to attack.

SAM HOUSTON'S PLAN WORKS

The army of Santa Anna was now over 7,000 strong. Houston's army still numbered less than 700. Instead of fighting the Mexicans, he tried to stay away from them. He zigzagged north, then east, then south, then west with his men. He would often get close enough to get a look at the Mexicans, then dart back away from them. Houston was waiting for Santa Anna to make a mistake.

It finally happened. Feeling sure of victory, the Mexican general gave the order for his advance army of about 1,300 men to have a hot meal and get some sleep. He put up a few guards, but they weren't as attentive as they should have been.

Houston and his men crept up closer and closer to the banks of the San Jacinto River, where the Mexicans had made their camp. Finally, less than 200 yards from the sleeping army, the Texans pounced. "Remember the Alamo!" they screamed. "Remember Goliad!"

The battle at San Jacinto was over in 18 minutes. The Mexican soldiers were groggy and confused, and could barely organize themselves to fight back. When the battle was over, 630 Mexicans were dead, and more than 700 were taken prisoner. Because Santa Anna was among the prisoners, the fighting was over. Texas had won its independence.

An injured Santa Anna surrenders to Houston.

THE SLOW ROAD TO STATEHOOD

The story of Texas doesn't end with the battle of San Jacinto, however. Texas had declared itself an independent republic. Sam Houston and Stephen Austin were elected as its leaders. Most of the Texans, however, still thought of themselves as Americans. What many of them really wanted was for Texas to be admitted into the Union as a state.

That didn't happen for nine years. The government of the United States was hesitant to invite Texas to become a state. For one thing, Americans were concerned that to do so would provoke a war with Mexico. The United States had no interest in such a war.

The issue of slavery, too, was a prickly one. Texas, as we mentioned earlier, allowed its farmers to own slaves. This caused problems in Congress. It took a vote by Congress to allow any new territory to become a state. The Northern states were against slavery, and their Congressmen wanted to vote against Texas. The Southern states sympathized with Texas, and wanted to vote for its statehood. Finally, after a long debate that went on for years, the vote went in favor of Texas. On December 19, 1845, during the presidency of John Tyler, Texas became the 28th state.

More and more settlers poured into Texas after it won its independence from Mexico.

Sam Houston was the first governor of the state of Texas. *(Art: University of Oklahoma.)*

A FINAL WORD

There would be many battles ahead for Texas. The United States did go to war with Mexico, as government leaders had predicted. The issue of slavery was an emotional one, which was finally decided in the American Civil War.

In all of the adversity, however, Texas endured. The pride and stubbornness the Texans had shown in settling and fighting for their beloved land kept them strong.

THE ALAMO

The building from which Davy Crockett, Jim Bowie, and others defended themselves against the Mexican army has become famous. Thousands of people every year visit the Alamo, restored in 1960 as a national landmark, in San Antonio, Texas. Many people are surprised to learn that the Alamo was built more than a century before the famous battle occurred there in 1836.

The Alamo was built in 1718 by a Spanish priest, Father Antonio Olivares. Olivares was a missionary who believed that it was his duty to bring his Catholic religion to the Indians of Mexico. What we know as the Alamo was built as a Catholic church, or mission, in San Antonio.

Olivares named his mission San Antonio de Valero, after a Spanish official in Mexico, the Marquis de Valero. It was from this mission that much of Olivares' work with the Mexican Indians took place. In those days, a mission or church was not just a place of worship on Sunday mornings. Rather, its space was used for classrooms for teaching the Spanish language, customs, and religion. There were also spaces for the Indians to learn spinning, sewing, farming, and carpentry.

The building was originally made of straw and sticks. As Spanish people continued to rule the territory, however, the mission was rebuilt in a more permanent way. When San Antonio de Valero was rebuilt, the Spanish government in Mexico agreed to help protect it from attack, providing it could also be used as a fortress.

The layout of the mission was not much different from other missions of the day. It had a large courtyard, or plaza, surrounded by a high wall. A ditch, running from north to south, was dug so that the mission would have fresh water from the San Antonio River.

The Alamo: army barracks (left foreground), courtyard (left background), and the church (right).

The ditch ran through the plaza.

San Antonio de Valero had a chapel made of stone, as well as a living space for the priests. The living space was also made of stone. The main entry of the mission was on the south side. There were areas inside the mission for such necessary occupations as leather tanning and blacksmithing.

By the end of the 18th century, however, the mission had changed. The plans of making the area a large Spanish settlement had failed. Spanish people who lived in the area preferred to live farther south, closer to the large cities of Mexico. Most of the Indians grew bored with the priests' attempts to make them "good Spanish citizens." They no longer came to the mission to learn crafts, religion, or a new language. By 1800, San Antonio de Valero was completely deserted.

The abandoned mission came to life once more in 1810. It was then that the Mexican Indians began fighting off the Spanish settlers. The Mexicans no longer wanted to be ruled by Spain, and they waged a fierce and bloody war. Some of the Spanish soldiers used the mission as living space and headquarters while they were fighting the Mexican Indians. They renamed the place "Pueblo del Alamo," which means "Alamo village" in Spanish. *Alamo* is the Spanish word for cottonwood trees, and there were lots of those around the building! For short, the mission-turned-fort was simply called the Alamo.

The Alamo went through a roller-coaster ride of vacancy and occupation in the next years. For a while it was used by the Mexican army trying to drive out the American settlers in Texas. In 1835, an army of 300 men attacked the Alamo, and drove out the Mexican army stationed there.

The victory was too easy, however. The Texans took over the Alamo, changing the layout of the place. They added a fort hospital and more barracks for the Texas army. On March 6, the 188 men inside the Alamo were attacked by General Santa Anna and his army of 5,000 men. The Texans' defeat at the Alamo was the rallying cry for outraged Americans who wanted revenge: "Remember the Alamo!"

IN THE DAYS OF THE TEXANS

1519	First Spanish explorers map Texas coast.
1620	The English ship *Mayflower* lands in Massachusetts.
1690	First mission established by Spanish priests in east Texas.
1732	George Washington is born in the Virginia territory.
1787	The U. S. Constitution is signed.
1790	The U.S. population is 3,929,214.
1794	The first U.S. silver dollar is minted.
1802	America's first real hotel is built in Saratoga, New York.
1803	Explorers Lewis and Clark set off on their expedition to see lands recently purchased from France.
1808	Congress prohibits African slave trade.
1821	Stephen Austin leads the Old Three Hundred to Texas.
1828	*Webster's Dictionary of the English Language* published.
1835	Texas' revolution begins.
1836	Texas' army slaughtered at the Alamo.
1837	First women's college, Mount Holyoke, opens its doors.
1845	Texas becomes 28th state.
1850	California joins the Union.
1851	Maine passes a law prohibiting the sale of liquor.
1851	First condensed milk is produced.
1852	*Uncle Tom's Cabin* published.
1852	First intercollegiate rowing match held, between Yale and Harvard.
1866	First big cattle drive takes place, from Texas to Kansas and Missouri.
1867	United States purchases Alaska from Russia.
1874	Santa Anna dies in Mexico City.
1960	The Alamo becomes an official national historic landmark.

COLOMA PUBLIC LIBRARY